Biomes
of North
America

A Journey into a Wetland

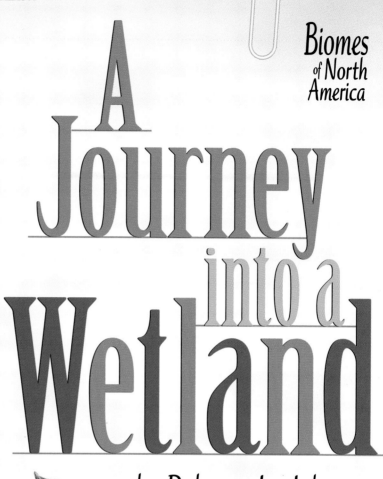

by Rebecca L. Johnson

with illustrations by Phyllis V. Saroff

CAROLRHODA BOOKS, INC./MINNEAPOLIS

Carolrhoda Books, Inc.
A division of Lerner Publishing Group
241 First Avenue North
Minneapolis, Minnesota 55401 U.S.A.

Website address: www.lernerbooks.com

Library of Congress Cataloging-in-Publication Data

Johnson, Rebecca L.
    A journey into a wetland / by Rebecca L. Johnson ; with
illustrations by Phyllis V. Saroff.
      p.   cm. — (Biomes of North America)
    Summary: Takes readers on a walk in a swamp, showing
examples of how the animals and plants of wetlands are connected
and dependent on each other and the wetland's watery
environment.
    ISBN: 1-57505-593-7 (lib. bdg. : alk. paper)
    1. Wetland ecology—Juvenile literature. 2. Wetlands—Juvenile
literature. [1. Wetland ecology. 2. Wetlands. 3. Ecology.] I. Saroff,
Phyllis V., ill. II. Title. III. Series.
    QH541.5.M3J64 2004
    577.68—dc22   2003015091

Manufactured in the United States of America
1 2 3 4 5 6 - JR - 09 08 07 06 05 04

Words to Know

ALGAE (AL-jee)—plantlike living things that use sunlight to make their own food

BACTERIA (bak-TEE-ree-uh)—microscopic, one-celled living things found almost everywhere

BOG—a low-lying spongy wetland found in cool climates where the most common plant is peat moss

DECOMPOSER—a living thing that breaks down dead plants, animals, and other natural wastes and returns their valuable nutrients to the environment

FOOD CHAIN—the connection among living things that shows what eats what in an ecosystem

LARVAE (LAR-vee)—pre-adult forms of animals

MARSH—a wetland where most of the plants are grasses

PRAIRIE POTHOLE—a small, marshlike wetland found on the flat prairie landscape

PREDATOR (PREH-duh-tur)—an animal that hunts and eats other animals

PREY (PRAY)—an animal that is hunted and eaten by other animals

SWAMP—a forested wetland

WATER BIOME (BYE-ohm)—a major community of living things in a water-based area

WETLAND—an area of land that is covered by shallow water all or part of the year

Long shadows
on still water

A craggy-nosed alligator snoozes on the muddy bank.
The air is warm and damp. Birds call from the
treetops. Insects flit in and out of the shadows.

 Splash! The alligator's eyes snap open. Wide
awake—and hungry—she slinks into the water. Here
in the swamp, the hunt is on.

5

A swamp is a dark, drippy place where land and water intertwine. It is full of creatures that slither and screech and splash. All life here is tied to the water that winds its way slowly around tree trunks and patches of squishy mud.

A swamp is a type of wetland. A wetland is land that is covered with shallow water for all or part of the year. Some wetlands stretch for miles and miles. Other wetlands are no bigger than a playground or parking lot.

Shallow water surrounds the bases of tall trees in a swamp (left). The Florida Everglades (below) are one of North America's largest wetlands.

Water biomes range from fast-flowing rivers (above) and ever-changing estuaries (left) to the salty ocean that covers nearly 75 percent of the earth's surface (below).

Perhaps you've seen a wetland. You've probably walked beside a river or a lake. You may have gone to the ocean or even seen an estuary. Estuaries form in places where rivers meet the ocean.

Wetlands, along with lakes, rivers, estuaries, and the ocean, make up the earth's water biomes. A water biome is a water-based region that is home to a unique group of living things. These living things are all adapted, or specially suited, to living in that region.

Each biome's living things, from tiny microscopic creatures to large plants and animals, form a community. Each member of that community depends on the others. All these living things, in turn, depend on the water—fresh or salty, moving or still—that forms their watery home. They swim through it, find food in it, and are carried from place to place by it. Without the water, they could not survive.

A raccoon feasts on a freshly caught trout.

Slender roots dangle from the pinhead-sized leaves of duckweed—tiny marsh plants that float on the water's surface.

The water in a wetland can come from rain, melted snow, or an underground spring. It can also spill over from another water biome, such as a lake or a river.

Different kinds of wetlands are named for the most important types of plants that live in them. A marsh is a grassy wetland where softly swaying reeds and cattails grow in shallow water. A good place to look for a marsh is near a river or around the edges of lakes and ponds.

Ducks paddle around the tall grasses that grow in a marsh.

A prairie pothole is a specific type of marsh. It is a small dip in a flat prairie that fills with water from rain and melting snow. Each spring and summer, prairie potholes become homes for millions of ducks, geese, and other birds. These patches of grass and water are perfect places to build nests, lay eggs, and raise chicks.

A prairie pothole fills a low spot in the prairie landscape.

Sundews are insect-eating bog plants that trap their prey in drops of sticky goo.

The water in a bog (top) can be visible at the surface or hidden just beneath it. A pitcher plant (above) thrives in a bog's damp soil.

A bog is a low-lying, spongy wetland found in cool climates. The most common bog plant is peat moss. It grows to be only a few inches above the ground. Over time, peat moss forms a very thick, very soft mat. Walking across a bog is like walking on a mattress. The ground quivers with every step.

12

A swamp is a forested wetland, full of trees and shrubs. Much of the ground is covered by water. But how deep the water is depends on how much rain falls—or doesn't—during the year.

The water in the swamp where the alligator lives is several feet deep. The water flows so slowly that its surface is usually flat and still. But look—there's a ripple. The alligator is back. Let's follow her on a journey into the swamp.

Thickly growing trees cast deep shadows on the still waters of a swamp.

Cypress "knees" stick up above the water around a cypress tree and help its water-covered roots get air.

Many of the trees growing in the alligator's swamp are bald cypresses with broad-bottomed trunks.

The alligator glides through the water without making a sound. Tall trees tower over her. Their leafy tops crowd together overhead, blocking out much of the morning sun.

Some of the trees stand on patches of muddy ground. Others seem to grow right out of the dark water that flows slowly through the swamp.

The biggest trees are bald cypresses. Their trunks flare out at the bottom. Clumps of Spanish moss hang from their branches like silvery gray gauze. The alligator stops at the base of a huge cypress tree. Only her eyes and the tip of her nose show above the water's surface.

Spanish moss (right) *absorbs water and nutrients from the air. The alligator* (below) *is a powerful—and fast—swimmer.*

A cluster of marsh marigold flowers makes a natural bouquet (left). Sweet nectar in the curved "tails" of jewelweed flowers (below) attracts bees and other insects that help the plant make seeds.

Other trees—such as black gum, tupelo, and water oak—grow among the cypresses. Twisting vines scramble through their branches, making a tangle of green.

Spicebush, pawpaw, and wax myrtle nestle in the shadows of the trees. Marsh marigolds and jewelweeds hug the damp ground. Their bright flowers light up the dark corners of the swamp.

Trees, bushes, and other swamp plants sink their roots deep into the black, slimy mud that lies around and beneath the water. The mud has a sour, musty odor.

On a patch of high ground, cypress knees sprout from the muddy swamp floor.

A skunk cabbage attracts insects to its flowers with a stinky odor instead of sweet nectar.

Nutrients in muddy swamp soil help young plants grow quickly.

When plants and animals that live in the swamp die, their remains end up in the mud. Worms, bacteria, and other decomposers break down these wastes. In the process, they return nutrients to the mud. Swamp plants need nutrients to live and grow.

Plantlike algae live in the water and on the mud. Some types of algae form a slimy, green scum that coats tree trunks, fallen branches, and rocks. Like plants, algae use sunlight to make their own food. Plants and algae are eaten by many swamp creatures. They are the first link in the swamp's food chain.

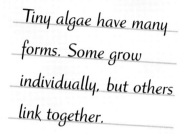

Tiny algae have many forms. Some grow individually, but others link together.

Bright green algae form a green scum on the water in part of the swamp.

19

When an alligator dives underwater, a clear protective membrane slides across each eyeball. They are like swim goggles.

The alligator scans the edge of the water. A jewel-colored dragonfly zooms past on broad, glistening wings. But nothing else moves. With a twitch of her powerful tail, the alligator disappears beneath the water's surface and sinks down to the muddy bottom. She waits, out of sight, for a meal to come her way.

A green darner dragonfly takes a break from flying (right). With her toothy jaws ready, the alligator prepares to slip beneath the water's surface (below).

Mosquito larvae are able to breathe underwater through little "snorkels" at the ends of their bodies.

The alligator's claws sink into the soft mud, disturbing three tiny clams that were half-buried in the ooze. A fat snail with a spiral shell creeps past the alligator's tail. With a tiny, rough tongue, the snail scrapes algae off a rock.

A shiny black diving beetle darts from behind a sunken log to snare a young salamander to eat. Later, the beetle gulps down a few mosquito larvae. The water is teeming with these tiny creatures. Some will avoid underwater predators long enough to leave the water and change into adult mosquitoes. The females will fly through the swamp in search of warm-blooded animals to bite.

A diving beetle holds a young salamander tightly in its powerful jaws.

Crayfish build mud "chimneys" around the entrances of their underground burrows to keep the water out.

Crayfish scurry around on the muddy swamp bottom. They daintily pick at sunken leaves and algae.

Silvery shiners and spotted swamp darters flit from one underwater hiding place to another. These tiny fishes are a favorite food of bigger fishes—bass and perch—that live in the swamp.

A crayfish waves its big claws as a warning—keep away or risk being pinched!

Not far from the resting alligator, there's a bump in the muddy bottom. But wait—the "bump" has eyes! It's a snapping turtle.

The snapping turtle is a patient hunter. It hides in the mud for hours at a time, waiting for a fish or crayfish to wander within reach of its sharp beak.

The hook at the end of a snapping turtle's beak is perfect for snagging a passing meal.

With the help of long barbels, a catfish finds its way (right). The long, narrow jaws of a garfish (below) bristle with needle-sharp teeth.

Soon a small catfish appears, cruising slowly above the mud. Long barbels stick out from its face like whiskers on a cat. The barbels help the fish feel its way through the murky water. The catfish suddenly stops. It senses that the alligator is near. The fish turns and starts to swim away.

But the catfish doesn't notice the long-nosed garfish that has come up from behind. With lightning speed, the garfish strikes.

The struggling fish attract the alligator's attention. She surges toward them across the muddy swamp bottom. Her jaws snap shut on a two-fish meal!

The alligator sends water flying as she grabs the two fish.

Frogs hatch from eggs as legless tadpoles with long tails. As tadpoles grow, they sprout legs and lose their tails.

The swamp is an ideal home for a frog. It is damp and dark and full of insects to eat.

The alligator thrashes in the water as she gulps down the fish. A big-eyed frog kicks hard to get out of the way. It leaps out of the water onto a fallen log.

The frog nearly lands on a four-toed salamander. The startled salamander dives into a hole in the log. It peers out from its hiding place with bulging eyes.

On top of the log, a pair of yellow-bellied pond sliders bask in a patch of sunlight. Like most other turtles, pond sliders love to sun themselves.

Turtles may be slow on land. But if danger threatens, they can slide into the water in a flash.

Grab a four-toed salamander by the tail, and the tail will break off—a trick that helps the salamander escape predators.

When a cottonmouth strikes, it injects poison into its prey with large teeth called fangs.

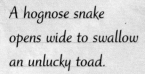

A hognose snake opens wide to swallow an unlucky toad.

The alligator swims past the log and heads for a muddy bank. Her wet, scaly skin glistens in the sunlight as she lumbers out of the water. She plods through strange, swirling tracks in the mud. They were made by a snake that slithered past several hours ago.

The track maker may have been a brown water snake that was chasing a mouse. It could have been a hognose snake following a toad. Or perhaps it was a deadly cottonmouth chasing another snake.

Farther along the bank is a big mound of branches and dead leaves. The alligator crawls on top of the mound. With her front legs, she carefully scrapes away a layer of brown leaves.

The mother alligator guards her nest carefully. If anything comes too close, she will hiss and then charge.

A dozen white eggs are clustered in the middle of the mound. They are the alligator's eggs. In just a few days, they will hatch.

Inside the alligator's nest are dozens of eggs (right). A baby alligator squirms out of its leathery shell (below).

The mother alligator will take good care of her young. She will bring them fish and other food to eat. She will gently pick them up in her huge, toothy mouth and carry them from place to place. When she takes them swimming, she'll even let them ride on her back and head.

Baby alligators eat insects, worms, and small fish. They will stay with their mother for about eighteen months.

A woodpecker has an amazingly long tongue that it uses to reach insects in the holes it drills. Inside the bird's head, the tongue wraps around the skull and is anchored at the base of the bill.

A sharp-eyed red-bellied woodpecker scans the bark of a tree for insects.

The alligator stretches out beside her nest. The afternoon sun is high in the sky. It beats down on the swamp, making the still air feel heavy and hot. The alligator closes her eyes for a nap. Other swamp animals, though, are wide awake. Bluebottle flies buzz near the water's edge. A frog croaks. There's the sharp call—*chink!*—of a waterthrush. Somewhere in the treetops overhead a prothonotary warbler is singing *zweet, zweet, zweet.* And from the distance comes the steady hammering of a red-bellied woodpecker.

The swamp, like other kinds of wetlands, is home to great numbers of birds. Birds build their nests in the swamp's trees and shrubs. They dine on fish and snails from the water. They snatch insects from the air and eat the fruits and seeds of swamp plants.

A prothonotary warbler (above) heads toward its nest with dinner in its beak. With mouths open wide, waterthrush chicks (right) beg for food from one of their parents.

Wood ducklings
pause at the edge
of their nest before
the big jump.

*In a quiet part of the
swamp, a male wood
duck rests in a patch
of water lilies.*

A pair of wood ducks flies in and lands on the water. With heads down and tails up, they search the bottom for crayfish and water bugs.

Wood ducks lay their eggs in holes in the trunks of trees that overhang the water. Just one day after hatching, the ducklings leave the nest—by leaping out of the tree trunk into the water below!

The curved tips of a limpkin's beak help it extract snails from their shells.

Not far from the sleeping alligator, a limpkin walks along the water's edge. Every now and then, it stops to plunge its long beak deep into the mud. The limpkin is searching for snails—its favorite food.

A purple gallinule strides past on long legs—and even longer toes. It is hunting for insects and frogs.

The long, widespread toes of a gallinule help it to walk on water lily leaves without sinking.

Elegant in pure white, a great egret hunts for fish beneath towering trees in the swamp.

A great egret slowly stalks through the shallows. Its sharp eyes scan the water. The slightest ripple could reveal a fish or frog. The egret uses its feet to feel for snails, crayfish, and baby turtles hiding in the mud.

Farther out in the water, a glossy black anhinga has just come up from a dive. It holds a small fish in its spear-shaped bill. With a flip of its head, the bird tosses the fish up and swallows it whole.

Few fish are fast enough to escape an anhinga's sharp bill.

Unlike duck feathers, the feathers of anhingas aren't waterproof. After diving, an anhinga spreads its wings to dry out its wet feathers.

A swamp rabbit munches a vine. Swamp rabbits are good swimmers. When chased by a predator, they often dive into the water to escape.

Hours pass. Long shadows slowly creep over the swamp as daylight turns to dusk. In the fading light, birds fly off to nests and perches in the trees. A hush falls over the swamp.

Two long, furry ears twitch above a clump of jewelweed. A swamp rabbit has arrived. It's been resting in a hollow log all day. Now that the sun is setting, it has come out to nibble tender leaves and shoots and drink at the water's edge.

Soft splashing sounds come from a few feet away.
A raccoon is hunched beside the water. With its
sensitive front paws, it searches in the shallows for
clams, worms, and crayfish.

*A raccoon uses its
front paws to feel for
worms and other
small creatures hidden
in the soft mud.*

High overhead, a white shape moves along a tree branch. It's an opossum, out looking for food. The opossum's nose twitches as it catches the scent of a bird's eggs.

Opossums have a prehensile, or grasping, tail. With its tail, an opossum can hang from a branch, leaving all four paws free.

A young opossum hitches a ride on its mother's back as she climbs through the treetops.

From its perch high in a tree, a barred owl scans the swamp below.

Suddenly, the opossum flattens itself against the branch. A barred owl swoops silently past. The owl glides down over the water, scanning the edge for mice and crayfish. It flies up to the top of an old cypress and calls out *who-who-who-whooooo.*

As these paw prints show, bobcats can retract, or pull in, their claws when they aren't using them.

claws out

claws retracted

Bobcats aren't afraid to get wet. They will plunge into the water for a meal of fish.

Other hunters are also prowling through the swamp. A bobcat pads softly around the trees, leaping over the water from one patch of ground to another.

Like a shadow, a fox slinks closer to the water. It spies the swamp rabbit drinking.

Without a sound, the fox inches closer to the rabbit. Its muscles tense. At the last moment, the rabbit senses danger. As the fox springs, the rabbit leaps into the water with a big splash and swims off into the darkness.

The fox stops at the water's edge. There may be easier meals to find farther along the bank. The fox moves on. It comes to the alligator's nest. The alligator is nowhere to be seen.

Poised at the water's edge, the fox watches its missed meal get away.

With teeth bared, the mother alligator rushes in to protect her nest.

The scent of eggs reaches the fox's keen nose.
The fox climbs the mound and begins to dig.
   With a roar, the alligator leaps out of the water.
The fox springs backward just as the alligator's jaws
snap shut. The fox sprints off into the trees.
Overhead there's a flurry of wings as a startled bird
wakes up.

Morning mists swirl among the cypress trees as a new day dawns in the swamp.

Still hissing, the alligator inspects her nest. The eggs are safe. She covers them with leaves again and lies down next to the nest. She will keep a close watch until dawn, when the morning light will chase away the nighttime hunters and bring a new day to the swamp.

for further
Information
about Wetlands

Books

Arnosky, Jim. *Wild and Swampy.* New York: HarperCollins, 2000.

Collard III, Sneed B. *Our Wet World.* Watertown, MA: Charlesbridge Publishing, 1998.

Cone, Molly. *Squishy, Misty, Damp and Muddy.* San Francisco: Sierra Club Books, 1996.

George, Jean Craighead. *Everglades.* New York: HarperCollins, 1995.

Gibbons, Gail. *Marshes & Swamps.* New York: Holiday House, 1998.

Greenaway, Theresa. *Look Closer: Swamp Life.* New York: Dorling Kindersley, 2000.

Grimm, Phyllis W. *Crayfish.* Minneapolis: Lerner Publications, 2001.

Kudlinski, Kathleen V. *Venus Flytraps.* Minneapolis: Lerner Publications, 1998.

Lourie, Peter. *Everglades: Buffalo Tiger and the River of Grass.* Honesdale, PA: Boyds Mills Press, 1998.

Luenn, Nancy. *Squish! A Wetland Walk.* New York: Atheneum, 1994.

Sayres, Meghan Nuttall. *The Shape of Betts Meadow: A Wetlands Story.* Brookfield, CT: Millbrook Press, 2002.

Silver, Donald M. *Swamp.* New York: McGraw-Hill, 1997.

Simon, Seymour. *Crocodiles & Alligators.* New York: HarperCollins, 1999.

Staub, Frank. *Alligators.* Minneapolis: Lerner Publications, 1995.

Staub, Frank. *Herons.* Minneapolis: Lerner Publications, 1997.

Winner, Cherie. *Salamanders.* Minneapolis: Carolrhoda Books, 1993.

Yolen, Jane. *Welcome to the River of Grass.* New York: Putnam Publishing Group, 2001.

Websites

Everglades National Park
< http://www.everglades.national-park
.com/ >

This site provides information on Everglades National Park, including planning a trip to the park.

Friends of the Everglades
< http://www.everglades.org/ >

On this site, you will find information on the Florida Everglades and on how you can help fight to protect one of the world's unique natural treasures.

U.S. Environmental Protection Agency—
* Wetlands*
< http://www.epa.gov/owow/wetlands/ >

This government agency's site provides information on what the government is doing to protect our wetlands.

U.S. Fish and Wildlife Service—National
* Wetlands Inventory*
< http://wetlands.fws.gov/ >

Another government agency website that links to cool sites for kids.

Photo Acknowledgments

The photographs in this book are used with the permission of: © James P. Rowan, pp. 4, 8 (bottom), 12 (bottom), 13, 16 (left and right), 19; Tom Stack & Associates (© Tom Stack, pp. 6, 14, 24 (bottom), 36; © Brian Parker, pp. 7, 8 (middle), 24 (top), 39; © Sharon Gerigs, pp. 8 (top), 10; © Joe McDonald, pp. 9, 20 (bottom), 22, 23, 26, 28, 41, 42; © Kevin Magee, p. 11; © Thomas Kitchin, pp. 12 (top), 34, 40; © Brian & Cyndy Parker, p. 15 (top); © Mark Allen Stack, pp. 15 (bottom), 35; © Mark Newman, p. 17; © Joe & Carol McDonald, p. 18; © Therisa Stack, p. 31; © Tom & Therisa Stack, p. 32; © Dawn Hire, p. 38; TSADO/USFWS, p. 45); Visuals Unlimited (© Dick Poe, p. 20 (top); © Gary Meszaros, p. 21; © Dale Jackson, p. 29; © Kirtley-Perkins, p. 30 (top); © Gary Carter, p. 33 (top); © Fritz Polking, p. 37); Photo Network (© Mark Sherman, p. 25; © David Davis, p. 44); © Sally McCrae Kuyper, p. 27; © Wendell Metzen/Bruce Coleman, Inc., p. 30 (bottom); © Rob & Ann Simpson/Photo Agora, p. 33 (bottom); © Anna Sullivan, p. 43.

Cover photographs by © Therisa Stack/Tom Stack & Associates.

Index

Numbers in **bold** refer to photos and drawings.